CORNERSTONES
OF FREEDOM™

The SPACE RACE

BY PETER BENOIT

CHILDREN'S PRESS®

An Imprint of Scholastic Inc.
New York Toronto London Auckland Sydney
Mexico City New Delhi Hong Kong
Danbury, Connecticut

BRINGING HISTORY to LIFE

Content Consultant
James Marten, PhD
Professor and Chair, History Department
Marquette University
Milwaukee, Wisconsin

Library of Congress Cataloging-in-Publication Data

Benoit, Peter, 1955–
  The space race/by Peter Benoit.
    p. cm.–(Cornerstones of freedom)
  Includes bibliographical references and index.
  Audience: Grades 4 to 6.
  ISBN-13: 978-0-531-23065-7 (lib. bdg.)   ISBN-10: 0-531-23065-1 (lib. bdg.)
  ISBN-13: 978-0-531-28165-9 (pbk.)   ISBN-10: 0-531-28165-5 (pbk.)
  1. Space race—History—Juvenile literature. 2. Astronautics—United
States—History—Juvenile literature. 3. Astronautics—Soviet
Union—History—Juvenile literature. 4. Space flight—History—Juvenile
literature. I. Title.
  TL793.B396 2012
  629.4'109046—dc23   2011031454

Printed in the United States of America 113
SCHOLASTIC, CHILDREN'S PRESS, CORNERSTONES OF FREEDOM™,
and associated logos are trademarks and/or registered trademarks of
Scholastic Inc.

 2 3 4 5 6 7 8 9 10 R 21 20 19 18 17 16 15 14 13 12

Photographs © 2012: Alamy Images/ITAR-TASS Photo Agency: 16; AP
Images: 39 (Bob Shutz), 8 (Diether Endlicher), 46, 54 (NASA), 23, 56; Getty
Images: 30 (Central Press/Hulton Archive), 4 top, 7 (Fox Photos), 41 (Lynn
Pelham/Time & Life Pictures), 12 (OFF/AFP), 22, 57 bottom (Terry Disney/
Central Press), 47 (Time & Life Pictures/NASA); NASA: cover, 48 (David R.
Scott), 2, 3, 33, 59 (James McDivitt), 49 (Marshall Space Flight Center), 11
(NACA), 55 (Smiley N. Pool/Houston Chronicle), back cover, 4 bottom, 7, 18,
20, 21, 25, 26, 28, 32, 34, 35, 36, 40, 43, 50; National Air and Space Museum,
Smithsonian Institution: 31; Newscom/N. Chmelevsky/ITAR-TASS: 29; Photo
Researchers/RIA Novosti/SPL: 38; Superstock, Inc./SSPL: 44; The Granger
Collection: 5 top, 6, 13; The Image Works/akg-images/RIA Novosti: 5 bottom

Did you know that studying history can be fun?

BRING HISTORY TO LIFE by becoming a history investigator. Examine the evidence (primary and secondary source materials); cross-examine the people and witnesses. Take a look at what was happening at the time—but be careful! What happened years ago might suddenly become incredibly interesting and change the way you think!

Contents

4

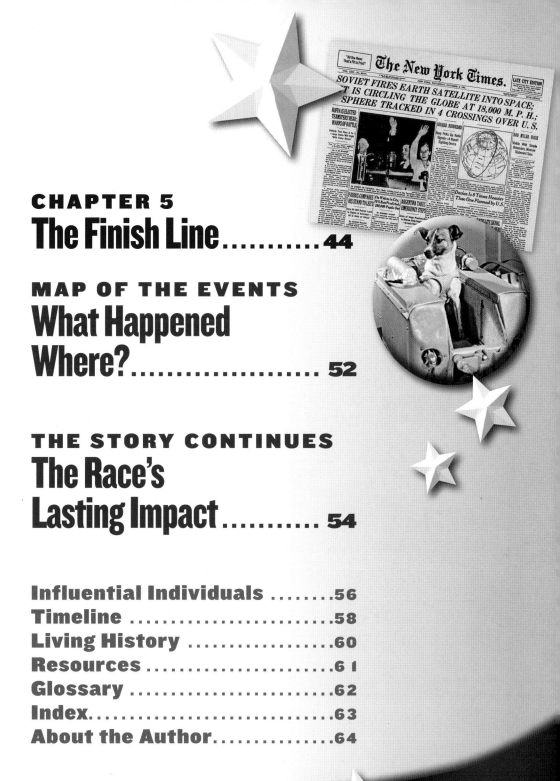

Cold War

The Treaty of Versailles brought an official end to World War I.

The world was involved in a bitter arms race from the earliest years of the 20th century. This competition to build bigger and more powerful weapons helped lead to World War I. The Treaty of Versailles brought the war to an unsteady peace in 1919. The arms race continued into World War II (1939–1945). Nazi Germany recruited engineers such as Wernher von Braun to study how the technology of **rockets** might be used to attack distant targets. These engineers eventually perfected a rocket called the V-2. It had a range of more than 100 miles (161 kilometers) and could carry a large bomb.

At the end of the war, the United States, the Soviet Union, and Great Britain scrambled for control of the engineers who had helped to create the rockets. Braun began working for the United States, which was focused on keeping rocket technology from falling into Soviet hands. An intense competition grew between the United States and the Soviet Union. The arms race became known as the Cold War. But the technological conflict also had a more scientific aspect—the space race.

V-2 rockets had the potential to cause massive damage from far away.

THE TREATY OF VERSAILLES.

CHAPTER 1

EARLY DEVELOPMENTS

German pilot Hans Guido Mutke claimed that he broke the sound barrier two years before Chuck Yeager's 1947 flight.

Rocket technology inspired

a dream of building airplanes that could travel faster than sound. A few pilots claimed to have traveled fast enough to break the sound barrier while falling from great heights. This meant traveling some 760 miles (1,223 km) per hour. But many people considered the goal impossible for a plane in level flight. Some had come close. During World War II, Germany built a rocket plane that traveled at 596 mph (960 kph). Around the same time, the British built a jet that traveled at 606 mph (975 kph). Such speeds would require more power than regular jet aircraft were capable of. The United States and the Soviet Union both began researching ways to use rocket technology to build faster aircraft.

Chuck Yeager nicknamed his jet after his wife.

Breaking the Sound Barrier

The U.S. Army Air Forces and the National Advisory Committee for Aeronautics (NACA) began working with Bell Aircraft in the closing months of World War II. They hoped to create a rocket-powered **supersonic** aircraft. On October 14, 1947, test pilot Chuck Yeager broke the sound barrier in the new X-1 plane.

The X-1 improved on previous efforts by the Germans and British by using more powerful rockets. It also had a shape that was designed to easily cut through the air. Yeager and the X-1 traveled at about 1.06 times the speed of sound, or **Mach** 1.06. But Yeager's flight also revealed the difficulties that future aircraft would face. Faster aircraft would experience dangerously high temperatures and gravitational pressure at these high speeds. These machines would require new designs and different materials to remain safe and functional.

Work progressed slowly. It would be six years before pilot Scott Crossfield traveled at Mach 2. Korean War veteran Iven Kincheloe flew above 100,000 feet (30 km) and into outer space on September 7, 1956. Less than three weeks later, test pilot Mel Apt crashed the Bell X-2 plane shortly after traveling at Mach 3. The loss did little to lower excitement for the new aircraft. Researchers responded by designing the rocket-powered North American X-15 space plane. It flew higher than

Only a few pieces of Mel Apt's Bell X-2 survived the crash.

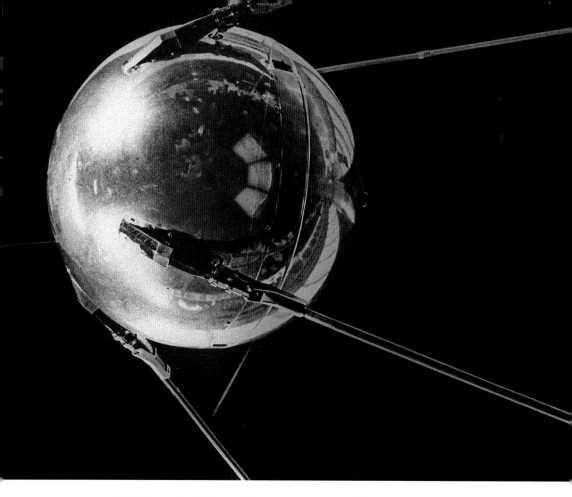

The launch of *Sputnik 1* sent waves of fear across the United States.

354,000 feet (108 km) and at almost Mach 7. But plans to develop a newer version of the X-15 were set aside after October 4, 1957.

The First Satellite

That day, the world learned that the Soviet Union had launched the world's first satellite, *Sputnik 1*. The satellite was the Soviet contribution to the International Geophysical Year (IGY). The IGY was sponsored by the National Academy of Sciences and lasted from July 1, 1957, to December 31, 1958. It was meant to reestablish sharing of scientific discoveries between the countries of the world. But *Sputnik* had the opposite effect. Alarmed Americans wondered whether the Soviets' ability to launch a satellite into **orbit** meant they could attack the

***Sputnik* made headlines around the world.**

A VIEW FROM ABR★AD

In 1959, then-senator John F. Kennedy's concern about America's falling reputation abroad was confirmed by polls taken in Great Britain, France, Norway, West Germany, and Italy. The results were reported in a classified document titled "Impact of U.S. and Soviet Space Programs on World Opinion." The report confirmed Kennedy's fears of "declining confidence in the U.S." It was leaked to the media. Coverage of the report increased public concern about Soviet attacks.

United States with nuclear warheads. Both the United States and the Soviet Union had pledged to launch satellites during the IGY. U.S. leaders were embarrassed that the Soviets had done it first.

The American response was swift and far-reaching. Senator John F. Kennedy expressed concern that the balance of power had been shifted in favor of the Soviets. The Soviet government was based on **communism**. Kennedy believed that *Sputnik* might make communism seem more appealing to leaders of third world countries. He was also less concerned about space exploration than the weapons that the Soviets could build using the new technology.

The Soviets planned to launch a second *Sputnik* satellite within a month of the first. Soviet engineer Sergei Korolyov had been watching the American media with interest. Before *Sputnik* ever launched, he had

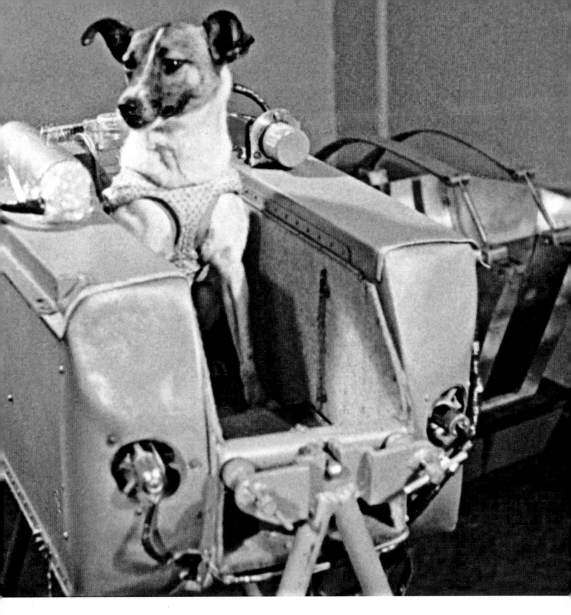

Laika survived only a few hours in space aboard *Sputnik 2*.

noted the resistance to spending millions of dollars for a satellite launch. So he convinced Soviet premier Nikita Khrushchev to go ahead with *Sputnik 1*. When talk turned to a second launch, Korolyov pressed Khrushchev to place a dog named Laika inside the satellite. Korolyov hoped Laika would help scientists

Sergei Korolyov

Sergei Korolyov was born in the Ukraine on January 12, 1907. Korolyov was a brilliant aircraft designer. He was arrested and imprisoned in 1938 for using government funds to advance rocket research. He spent the next six years in prison. Korolyov was assigned to a research laboratory in the prison. There, he worked alongside other scientists who had been imprisoned by Soviet leader Joseph Stalin. Korolyov worked for the Soviet space program after his release from prison. But his years in prison and his heavy workload ruined his health. He was advised by doctors to rest, but he worked harder instead. Korolyov died on January 14, 1966.

learn more about the safety of spaceflight for humans. Laika's journey was also a **propaganda** tool. Laika would become the first living creature to be sent into space. The Soviets claimed victory over the United States in the press when *Sputnik* 2 launched on November 3, 1957. However, Laika died shortly after liftoff. Soviet leaders admitted the dog had died during the mission, but implied it happened much later in the mission.

America's Response

The United States hoped to restore national pride by launching a satellite of its own. The attempted satellite launch on December 6 ended in embarrassment when a rocket failed a second after ignition. It exploded on the launchpad. The press responded by calling the failed launch "Flopnik." President Dwight Eisenhower's judgment was called into question. He had denied a request from Wernher von Braun to use the new Jupiter-C rocket that he and his team had developed. Eisenhower feared that using a military weapon in a peacetime mission would send the wrong message to a tense world. Now he realized that the nation's image abroad was at stake.

The United States used Braun's Jupiter-C rocket to launch the *Explorer 1* satellite on January 31, 1958. The successful launch began to restore the nation's wounded pride. On October 1, 1958, NACA was reorganized and expanded to include space exploration. It was renamed the National Aeronautics and Space Administration (NASA). The space race had begun.

Explorer 1 launched from Cape Canaveral, Florida.

CHAPTER 2

HUMANS IN SPACE

President Dwight Eisenhower (center) appointed the first leaders of NASA in 1958.

U.S. LEADERS SAW THE SPACE race as a way to prove the nation's strength. They hoped to show that the United States had greater scientific and military abilities than the Soviet Union. They also hoped to prove that communism was not as effective as U.S. democracy. Space exploration led to the development of more powerful rockets. This in turn raised the threat of long-range missiles, satellites, and other powerful weapons. Space exploration became closely linked to military strength. As a result, NASA supported missile technology instead of focusing on aircraft design. Missiles showed greater promise for military applications as well as for putting a man in space before the Soviets could.

The Project Mercury astronauts were selected carefully to meet NASA's needs.

Project Mercury Begins

In February 1959, NASA awarded McDonnell Aircraft the contract to build the first manned satellite. They named the satellite *Mercury*. The *Mercury* spacecraft was about 6 feet (1.8 meters) wide and simple in design. It could not change its path. NASA began testing hundreds of astronaut applicants for the newly created Project Mercury. They looked for highly intelligent college graduates who were test pilots. *Mercury*'s small size placed limits on which astronauts could fit inside. No astronaut could be more than 5 feet 11 inches (180 centimeters) tall or weigh more than 180 pounds (81.6 kilograms). Seven men were selected for the project: Scott Carpenter, Gordon Cooper, John Glenn, Virgil "Gus" Grissom,

Walter "Wally" Schirra, Alan Shepard, and Donald "Deke" Slayton. NASA tested the *Mercury* spacecraft and the rocket system that would launch it into space throughout 1960 and early 1961.

Sergei Korolyov realized that putting the first man in space would be a major propaganda victory. The Soviets began testing a spacecraft of their own named *Vostok*. The Soviet craft was round and slightly bigger than *Mercury*. It would use a rocket similar to the ones used in the successful *Sputnik* launches. The Soviets also began their own review of test pilots. They eventually selected Yuri Gagarin as their first cosmonaut, as astronauts were known in the Soviet Union. More than half of *Vostok*'s test launches had ended in failure. But the Soviets sent Gagarin into orbit on April 12, 1961. The mission went

YESTERDAY'S HEADLINES

NASA's Marshall Space Flight Center is located in Huntsville, Alabama. This made the *Huntsville Times* the unofficial news source for Project Mercury. The newspaper announced Yuri Gagarin's historic accomplishment of being the first man in space on April 12, 1961. It ran other articles on its front page that detailed NASA's frustration that the Soviets had put the first man in space. These articles had headlines such as "So Close, Yet So Far."

perfectly. Gagarin landed safely back on Earth. He was the first man to visit space. The Soviets had won a major victory in the propaganda war.

NASA engineers could not have been more disappointed. Three years of intense preparation had left them trailing the Soviets. NASA had carefully tested the Mercury astronauts on a device that imitated the motions they would encounter in space and had recorded their reactions. The *Mercury* spacecraft and the rocket that would launch it into space had been thoroughly prepared to perform a flawless mission. A chimpanzee named Ham had already been sent on a successful mission on January 31. But NASA engineers knew that they had once more been bested by the Soviets.

Yuri Gagarin became a national hero in the Soviet Union after his successful journey into space.

The First American in Space

On May 5, 1961, Alan Shepard and the *Freedom 7* capsule were launched into space by a Mercury-Redstone rocket. Unlike Gagarin, Shepard did not enter Earth's orbit. The capsule reached an **altitude** of more than 116 miles (187 km) and a maximum speed in excess of 5,000 mph (8,047 kph) before splashing down in the Atlantic Ocean 15 minutes later. Shepard and *Freedom 7* were recovered a short time later by the aircraft carrier USS *Lake Champlain*. Shepard received a congratulatory phone call from President John F. Kennedy. He

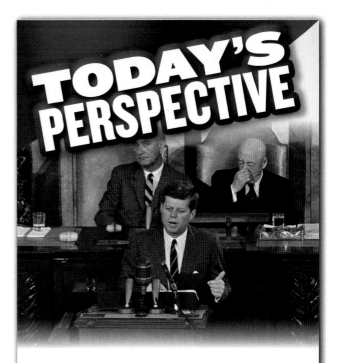

TODAY'S PERSPECTIVE

Yuri Gagarin's successful mission into space took place 23 days before the first Project Mercury launch. But Mercury was still a victory for the United States' space program. President John F. Kennedy gave a speech before Congress less than three weeks after the launch. He said, "I believe we should go to the Moon."

This new goal gave America's space program a new direction. Kennedy and his advisers knew that it would take many years to accomplish this goal. This would give the United States time to overtake the Soviet Union in the space race. Today, Alan Shepard's 1961 mission into space is seen as an important first step toward a much larger goal.

At 9:47 a.m. Eastern Standard Time on February 20, 1962, John Glenn became the first American astronaut to orbit Earth. The event captured the nation's imagination and made Glenn a hero. The launch was broadcast live on CBS News. See page 60 for a link to watch the broadcast online.

was also honored at a special ceremony three days later at the White House. Two weeks later, on May 25, Kennedy announced NASA's bold plan to put an American on the Moon by the end of the decade.

NASA's next launch on July 21 provided a reminder of the dangers faced by the Mercury astronauts. Virgil Grissom nearly drowned when the *Liberty Bell* 7 capsule began to fill with water after splashing down. Grissom made it out alive, but the spacecraft sank to the bottom of the Atlantic Ocean.

NASA finally accomplished its next major goal when John Glenn and the *Friendship* 7 spacecraft successfully orbited Earth on February 20, 1962. The mission was the triumph NASA had needed. Glenn became a national hero.

NASA was ready to repeat the success of Glenn's launch three months later. But astronaut Scott Carpenter experienced errors during the launch. He nearly ran out of fuel and landed 250 miles (402 km) away from his target. Carpenter left the program less than a year later. Wally Schirra got the Mercury program back on track in October 1962. He piloted the *Sigma* 7 spacecraft on a mission lasting more than nine hours. Schirra circled Earth six times. Gordon Cooper's 22-orbit flight aboard *Faith 7* the following May was the last Mercury mission. It also was a success.

The Soviets refused to be outdone. They launched a pair of *Vostok* spacecraft two days apart in June 1963. Cosmonaut Valentina Tereshkova piloted the second one. She was the first woman in space. Women were not allowed to become air force test pilots in the United States. This meant that they could not be astronauts. Tereshkova's mission was yet another propaganda victory for the Soviet Union. The United States had no answer for it. NASA would not select women astronauts until 1978. But both nations had their eyes fixed on the Moon. Neither the Americans nor the Soviets could dwell long on Tereshkova's achievement.

John Glenn's trip aboard *Friendship 7* was one of NASA's greatest victories in the early years of the space race.

CHAPTER 3

NEW DEVELOPMENTS

Faith 7 splashed down in the Pacific Ocean.

SOME NASA ENGINEERS supported another Mercury mission after Cooper's *Faith 7* capsule splashed down in May 1963. But President Kennedy's bold declaration before Congress had set the space race on a different path. The **lunar** mission called for new technologies that were still being planned and discussed. Rockets and spacecraft would need to be enlarged and given powerful new capabilities. In addition, descending to the surface of the Moon would require a self-sufficient spacecraft, or lunar module, that could separate and rejoin the main spacecraft, or command module. To do this, the lunar module needed **rendezvous** and **docking** capacities.

Rockets

Scientists predicted that the lunar mission might take as long as two weeks. It would require a crew rather than one astronaut. A *Gemini* capsule would carry two astronauts. It would need instruments that allowed its crew to use rockets to change orbit and dock with another spacecraft. A more powerful rocket would also be needed to launch the 8,000-pound (3,629 kg) *Gemini*.

The unmanned *Gemini* test rocket launched from Cape Kennedy, Florida.

NASA proposed a new mission of 10 flights during 1965 and 1966 to meet all of these goals. An unmanned test launch was completed in April 1964. The next proposed unmanned test mission was prevented by hurricanes until January 1965.

The Soviets had a plan of their own. They modified the spacecraft used for Vostok missions to make room for other cosmonauts.

Konstantin Feoktistov (left), Vladimir Komarov (center), and Boris Yegorov (right) were the three cosmonauts to travel aboard *Voskhod.*

On October 12, 1964, the new *Voskhod* craft carried three cosmonauts into orbit for one day. The Soviet government saw major changes while the cosmonauts were orbiting. Premier Nikita Khrushchev was overthrown. Leonid Brezhnev took his place.

A FIRSTHAND LOOK AT
THE FIRST SPACE WALK

A brief video clip of Alexei Leonov's space walk gives no sense of the difficulties he would face when he tried to reenter *Voskhod*'s air lock. The video shows Leonov floating effortlessly above Earth's surface. See page 60 for a link to view the video online.

Brezhnev hoped to establish a clear-cut advantage in the space race. The Soviets planned a bolder move for the upcoming *Voskhod 2* flight. The cosmonauts would participate in the first space walk ever. The decision would require the addition of an **air lock** to the *Voskhod* capsule. Without it, the cosmonauts would not be able to open the capsule's hatch in space. An inflatable air lock was attached to the side of the capsule. This raised the risk that the capsule might become unstable during reentry. The Soviets forged ahead anyway. They selected two cosmonauts, Alexei Leonov and Pavel Belyayev, for the mission.

Alexei Leonov's space walk represented the next leap forward in space exploration.

Walking in Space

On March 18, 1965, at the end of the first orbit of *Voskhod*'s mission, Leonov opened the hatch and climbed into the air lock. The 12-minute space walk began soon after. When Leonov attempted to reenter the air lock, he found that his stiff, bulky space suit and gloves had shifted on his body. This made him unable to fit through the air lock. He struggled as his air supply ran low. He worked his way inside at the last moment. He had survived what could have been a terrible accident.

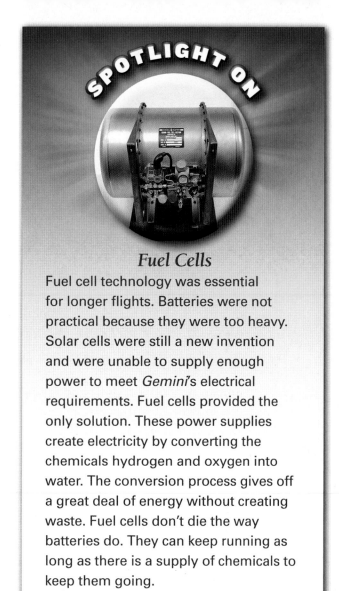

SPOTLIGHT ON

Fuel Cells

Fuel cell technology was essential for longer flights. Batteries were not practical because they were too heavy. Solar cells were still a new invention and were unable to supply enough power to meet *Gemini*'s electrical requirements. Fuel cells provided the only solution. These power supplies create electricity by converting the chemicals hydrogen and oxygen into water. The conversion process gives off a great deal of energy without creating waste. Fuel cells don't die the way batteries do. They can keep running as long as there is a supply of chemicals to keep them going.

However, *Voskhod*'s reentry did not go as planned. The capsule tumbled out of control and eventually landed in dense forests. The cosmonauts were rescued two days later. The drama of the mission revealed the dangers and difficulties of the space program. The Soviets would not send another man into orbit for two years.

NASA took full advantage of its chance to push ahead of the Soviets. It launched a manned Gemini mission piloted by Virgil Grissom and John Young on March 23, 1965. *Gemini 3* completed three orbits in five hours. Its success paved the way for a space walk on the next mission. *Gemini 4* was launched on June 3, 1965. Edward H. White II executed Gemini's first space walk during the four-day flight. It was a major step toward the longer mission that a lunar landing would require. It also showed that American astronauts had achieved a better understanding of spacewalking than the Soviets had.

James A. McDivitt (left) and Edward H. White II (right) manned the *Gemini 4* spacecraft.

James McDivitt photographed White's space walk.

NASA engineers knew that lunar missions presented problems other than those already solved. Longer missions would require larger amounts of electricity. To have any hope of reaching the Moon, future flights would need **fuel cells**. *Gemini 5* was the first flight to make use of fuel cells. But fuel cell technology was limited at the time. This barrier would have to be overcome.

TODAY'S PERSPECTIVE

Before the successful December 15, 1965, launch of *Gemini 6A* there had been another launch attempt. This attempt was ended when the spacecraft's computer accidentally began before liftoff. Command pilot Schirra (above) was left with a difficult decision. His training had taught him to eject from the spacecraft because there was a high risk of explosion. But tests of the ejection device had revealed that it might not be safe. Schirra also knew that ejecting would make it impossible for another launch to occur before *Gemini 7* had completed its mission. Schirra was criticized for disobeying his training. But his risk paid off when *Gemini 6A* launched safely a few days later.

NASA also planned to test the ability of *Gemini 6* to dock with another spacecraft. The mission was abandoned when the rocket that *Gemini 6* was supposed to dock with plummeted into the ocean. NASA officials had to change their plans to keep the project on track. They decided to put *Gemini 6A* and *Gemini 7* into orbit at the same time, where they would rendezvous. It was a daring plan. The *Gemini 7* launch took place on December 4, 1965. *Gemini 6A* was launched into orbit on December 15. The rendezvous of the two spacecraft went perfectly. *Gemini 7* spent 14 days in orbit. NASA had finally created a spacecraft that could stay in space for the length of a lunar mission.

The remaining Gemini missions were devoted to perfecting docking between two spacecraft. They were also used to help solve the difficulty of adapting to the zero gravity environment of a space walk. Spacewalking would allow astronauts to perform important tasks on the lunar mission. All of the testing and planning was finished by the end of the *Gemini 12* mission in November 1966. It was time for the Apollo lunar mission to begin. But there would be tragedy along the way.

Astronauts aboard *Gemini 6A* took photographs of *Gemini 7* as the two spacecraft successfully docked.

CHAPTER 4

TO THE MOON

The deaths of Gus Grissom (left), Edward White (center), and Roger Chaffee (right) raised public concern about the safety of spaceflight.

NASA BEGAN THE FINAL LEG of the space race with high hopes. The *Apollo 1* mission was to be little more than making sure everything worked properly, a process known as a systems check. But questions had arisen about the safety of the spacecraft even before routine preflight tests were scheduled. Gus Grissom, Edward White, and Roger Chaffee were the three astronauts chosen for the mission. They voiced their concerns, but tests went ahead as scheduled. A spark set the capsule ablaze in a test on January 27, 1967. The three men were killed in seconds.

Soyuz 1 **was manned by cosmonaut Vladimir Komarov, who had previously traveled aboard *Voskhod*.**

The Apollo Program

The nation had forgotten about the dangers of spaceflight after a string of 16 nearly flawless missions. People around the country were stunned by the news of the *Apollo 1* disaster. NASA responded by redesigning capsules to make such events less likely in the future. The Soviets launched their *Soyuz* spacecraft three months later. Cosmonauts had reported several design flaws to government leaders. They hoped to have the flight delayed until the problems could be corrected. Communist Party leaders would not listen. They planned to surpass the U.S. program after the *Apollo 1* disaster. *Soyuz 1* was doomed from the start. It fell to Earth and burst into flames on April 23 after 18 orbits.

Less than 10 months after the *Apollo 1* disaster, NASA sent the unmanned *Apollo 4* into orbit to test its heat shield. The heat shield would be necessary to protect future crews during reentry. It passed the test, and NASA engineers were free to move on to fine-tuning the new spacecraft's design. Its **navigation** and guidance systems were of particular interest. Full testing required another manned orbital mission. The 10-day mission launched on October 11, 1968. The new craft weighed 16 tons and was launched with a powerful Saturn 1B rocket. Both performed flawlessly.

A lunar module would be used to descend from

YESTERDAY'S HEADLINES

The shock of the *Apollo 1* disaster saddened the nation. Both the Senate and House called for investigations into the cause of the fire. Five astronauts (above) testified during the investigation. Groups of technical specialists were assembled to look into *Apollo 1* quality control and the failures of communication that led to the disaster. A full report was prepared for the Senate. It declared, "Safety is our prime consideration," and called for the creation of an Aerospace Safety Advisory Panel to improve project supervision and communication.

the orbiting *Apollo* command module to the surface of the Moon. Technical problems with the lunar module, however, forced NASA to change its plans. NASA engineers wanted to have a full rehearsal of the combined command module/lunar module system in Earth's orbit. But the lunar module was not ready in time. Instead, NASA engineers attached a dummy lunar module, called the Lunar Test Article, to the command module. This addition matched the weight of the missing lunar module and allowed the spacecraft to mimic what flight would be like with a lunar module. Astronauts Frank Borman, Jim Lovell, and William Anders were selected to pilot *Apollo 8*. On December 21, 1968, a colossal Saturn V rocket sent them on their way to the Moon.

 Apollo orbited Earth twice before

It took just over 69 hours for *Apollo 8* to reach lunar orbit.

Astronaut Jim Lovell's family watched the *Apollo 8* mission on television along with millions of other Americans.

setting out for its destination 240,000 miles (386,243 km) away. *Apollo* passed behind the Moon three days later. It settled smoothly into lunar orbit. It was Christmas Eve on Earth. More than a billion people followed the event on radio and television broadcasts. The three astronauts became instant celebrities after landing back on Earth three days later. But NASA scientists knew there was still work to be done before astronauts could walk on the Moon's surface.

A FIRSTHAND LOOK AT
THE MOON LANDING

The launch of *Apollo 11* captured the imagination of the world. The mission left a lasting impression of America's strength in space. It was a major propaganda victory in the Cold War. See page 60 for a link to view a video of the launch and the Moon landing.

NASA scheduled a full, manned orbital test of the lunar module and *Apollo 9* for March 3, 1969. The 10-day Earth orbit featured separation and docking of the *Apollo* command module. It tested the engines that the lunar module used to descend to and return from the lunar surface. The mission was a success.

NASA officials planned a lunar orbit with the command module and lunar module. Astronauts Tom Stafford, Gene Cernan, and John Young piloted the *Apollo 10* mission perfectly. The way was cleared for a lunar landing in July. People around the world looked forward to the event. They came to Cape Canaveral, Florida, to be a part of the historic event. The Soviets had seen their own lunar goals set aside by leaders of the Communist Party. They could only watch as American astronauts Neil Armstrong, Edwin "Buzz" Aldrin, and Michael Collins took center stage.

One Small Step

The July 16 launch of *Apollo 11* went perfectly. The flight itself was also without problems. The lunar module

Eagle began its descent when *Apollo 11* reached lunar orbit on July 20. *Eagle* tracked past its intended target and barely had enough fuel to complete a landing. Mission Control in Houston, Texas, heard Neil Armstrong say, "The *Eagle* has landed," once the lunar module was safely on the Moon's surface. Armstrong descended from the lunar module seven hours later. He spoke the famous words, "That's one small step for man, one giant leap for mankind," as he set foot on the Moon. Buzz Aldrin joined him moments later. The United States had reached a historic milestone and changed the world.

TODAY'S PERSPECTIVE

More than four decades have passed since the *Apollo 11* landing. The distance from it has given historians time to reflect on the meaning of the space race. Some have wondered whether the achievements in space exploration were worth the cost. Soviet premier Khrushchev barely reacted to President Kennedy's pledge to put a man on the Moon by the end of the decade. The Soviets instead directed their efforts to missile defense and a space station. On the other hand, some historians feel that hundreds of years from now, the 20th century will be remembered for mankind's exploration of space.

CHAPTER 5

THE FINISH LINE

Each of the *Apollo* spacecraft was launched into space by a Saturn V rocket.

THE *APOLLO 11* MISSION HAD been a great success. But NASA engineers were unhappy with the landing of the lunar module. Being unable to pinpoint landings could pose threats to safety in the future. Between 1966 and 1968, NASA had sent seven robotic spacecraft to the lunar surface to work out details of landing on the surface. Five touched down softly. NASA engineers decided to use one of them as a target for the *Apollo 12* lunar module landing. The November 1969 mission unfolded perfectly.

Apollo 13 splashed down in the Pacific Ocean on April 17, 1970.

The Apollo Program Continues

The *Apollo 13* launch in April 1970 was another matter. One of its engines failed shortly after liftoff. One of its oxygen tanks exploded two days later. The spacecraft was already more than halfway to the Moon. The explosion raised two problems. Oxygen was needed for the astronauts to breathe. It was also needed for the spacecraft's fuel cells to work. Commander Jim Lovell radioed Mission Control and said, "Houston, we've had a problem." The only option was to move to the lunar module, conserve electricity, and use the Moon's gravity to slingshot *Apollo* back to Earth. The three astronauts suffered from low temperatures and a lack of oxygen. But they managed to make it back to Earth safely.

NASA administrators examined *Apollo* to determine the cause of the explosion. Future missions would carry a reserve oxygen tank. Efforts to improve safety were only partly successful when *Apollo 14* lifted off on January 31, 1971. The lunar module's computer system almost caused it to cancel the lunar landing before pilot Joseph Engle brought it to rest near its target site. The lunar module operated flawlessly once it landed. Astronauts set up devices for scientific testing of the Moon. Information to be analyzed was streamed to Earth using radio communication. *Apollo 14* brought 94.5 pounds (43 kg) of lunar rock back to Earth. Scientific exploration of the Moon had begun.

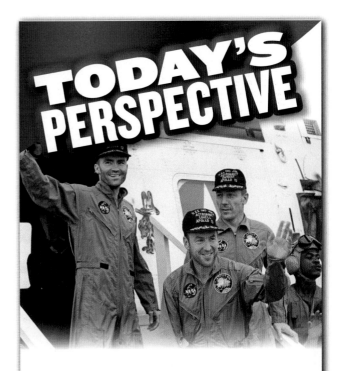

TODAY'S PERSPECTIVE

In 1970, the tense drama of the *Apollo 13* mission captured the attention of the world. The people of the United States watched and hoped for the astronauts' safe return. Newspapers and television broadcasts covered the event closely. There was a thorough investigation in the wake of the accident. Most experts now agree that it was the close cooperation of four dedicated directors at Mission Control and the three astronauts that kept the mission from becoming a tragedy. Careful problem solving brought the astronauts home safely.

Apollo 15 was launched on July 26, 1971. It represented a great leap forward for lunar research. Improvements to the lunar module allowed for longer stays on the lunar surface. A battery-powered vehicle called the Lunar Rover made broader exploration possible. Solar cells recharged the batteries. The Lunar Rover carried tools, rock samples, and cameras. Mission commander David Scott and lunar module pilot James Irwin collected 169 pounds (76.6 kg) of Moon rock, photographed the lunar surface, and examined gravity on the Moon.

The Lunar Rover helped the *Apollo 15* astronauts collect a variety of samples from the Moon.

The *Apollo 17* launch marked the end of an era.

The End of Apollo

Apollo 16 was launched on April 16, 1972. The Lunar Rover proved useful once again. Astronauts John Young and Charles Duke collected rock samples that helped scientists develop a better understanding of how the Moon's surface was formed. *Apollo 17* was the last mission of Project Apollo. It was launched on December 7, 1972. The mission spent more than three days on the lunar surface and collected 244 pounds (110.6 kg) of Moon rock.

The Skylab space station contained a variety of equipment to help astronauts conduct their studies.

NASA had already begun planning three additional *Apollo* missions. All three were abandoned in favor of an orbiting space station called Skylab, where several astronauts could live and work for weeks on end. The space station provided NASA an opportunity to study the effects of longer missions on astronauts' health. In addition, Skylab's telescopes gave scientists a more detailed understanding of the Sun than had previously been possible. Skylab supported three extended manned missions in 1973 and 1974.

A Peaceful Conclusion

By the 1970s, leaders in the Soviet Union and the United States sought ways to ease Cold War tensions between the two nations. The signing of the Helsinki Declaration in August 1975 called for the two countries to avoid threats and shows of force. It also called for them to find peaceful ways to resolve disputes. The space agencies of the two nations agreed to a joint mission called the Apollo-Soyuz Test Project. *Apollo* docked with the Soviet *Soyuz* spacecraft on July 17. Astronauts and cosmonauts conducted joint scientific experiments. They also exchanged gifts and shared meals. The space race had been born from Cold War tension. But it ended up being an important part of ending the conflict.

The impact of the space race extended far beyond this, though. Pictures of Earth taken from space gave a new focus to environmental concerns. The Space Race caused educators to focus more on math and science education. NASA's space program also has given rise to a large number of technological advancements.

A FIRSTHAND LOOK AT
THE *APOLLO-SOYUZ* DOCKING

The *Apollo-Soyuz* docking in July 1975 symbolized the end of Cold War tension. The whole world watched as the U.S. and Soviet space programs joined together for the first time. See page 60 for a link to watch a video of the docking online.

What Happened Where?

TX

Houston •

...uston, Texas
...SA's Mission Control is located here. This
...ility oversees every mission into space.

Gulf of Mexico

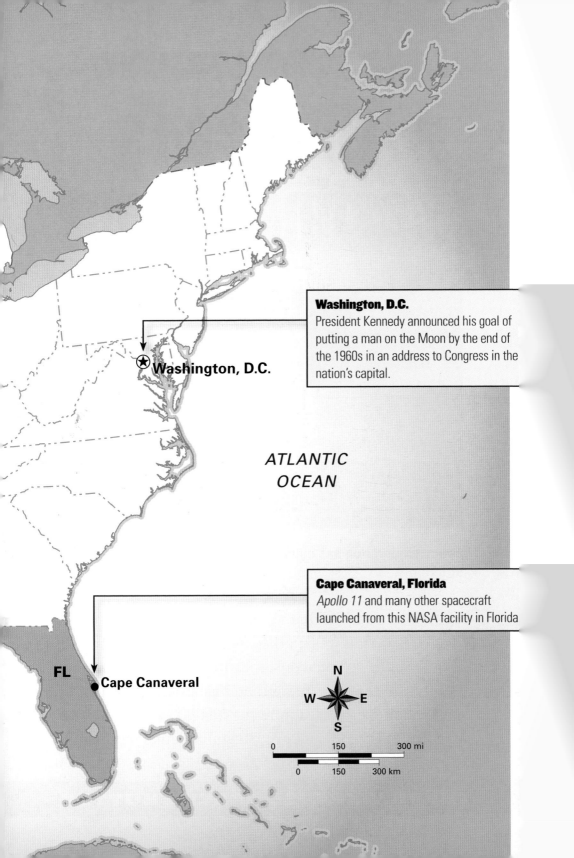

Washington, D.C.
President Kennedy announced his goal of putting a man on the Moon by the end of the 1960s in an address to Congress in the nation's capital.

⊛ Washington, D.C.

ATLANTIC
OCEAN

Cape Canaveral, Florida
Apollo 11 and many other spacecraft launched from this NASA facility in Florida

FL

● Cape Canaveral

N
W ✦ E
S

| 0 | 150 | 300 mi |
| 0 | 150 | 300 km |

The Race's Lasting Impact

Space exploration has caused many people to look at our planet differently.

The space race was one of the major symbols of the Cold War. The period was marked by economic competition, propaganda, and the constant threat of nuclear war. But the space race is more than just a part of the Cold War. It continues to capture the imagination to this day. Pictures of Earth rising over the lunar landscape had a powerful effect on environmental awareness around the world. The space race also caused a change in American education as people gained a new interest in math and science. This in turn fueled further technological growth. *Apollo*'s heat shield has led to advances in fire-resistant technologies for airplanes. Technologies such as freeze-dried foods, artificial limbs, hearing aids, and many others benefited from the space race.

The impact of the space race is just as great as the 20th century's wars, movements of social protest, or broad cultural changes. It stands as a symbol of human curiosity. Even today, NASA and other worldwide organizations seek to explore the limits of outer space.

The final mission of the space shuttle program launched on July 8, 2011.

MISSIONS BETWEEN 1981 AND 2011.

NFLUENTIAL INDIVIDUALS

Nikita Khrushchev (1894–1971) was the Soviet premier who supported the Soviet space program.

Sergei Korolyov (1907–1966) was the chief designer of the Soviet space program.

Wernher von Braun (1912–1977) was a German engineer who began working for the United States after World War II. He led the team that developed the Jupiter-C rocket.

John F. Kennedy

John F. Kennedy (1917–1963) was the 35th president of the United States. He promoted the idea of putting an American on the Moon before the 1960s had come to an end.

John Glenn (1921–) was the first American to orbit Earth.

Alan Shepard (1923–1998) was the United States' first man in space.

Chuck Yeager (1923–) was an American test pilot who was the first person to break the sound barrier.

Neil Armstrong (1930–) was the first man to walk on the lunar surface.

Edwin "Buzz" Aldrin (1930–) was part of the *Apollo 11* mission. He was the second man ever to walk on the Moon.

Yuri Gagarin (1934–1968) was a Soviet cosmonaut. He was the first man to orbit Earth.

Alexei Leonov (1934–) was a Soviet cosmonaut. He was the first man to complete a space walk.

Valentina Tereshkova (1937–) was a Soviet cosmonaut. She was the first woman in space.

Chuck Yeager

Yuri Gagarin

TIMELINE

1947

Chuck Yeager breaks the sound barrier.

1957

Sputnik is launched, beginning the space race.

1958

January
The United States launches its first satellite, *Explorer 1.*

October
NASA is formed.

1962

February 20
John Glenn becomes the first American to orbit Earth.

1963

June
Valentina Tereshkova becomes the first woman in space.

1965

March 18 Alexei Leonov completes the first space walk.

June 3 Edward White II performs the first American space walk.

1968

December
Apollo 8 completes a successful lunar orbital mission.

1969

July
Apollo 11 completes the first lunar landing mission.

July 20
Neil Armstrong and Buzz Aldrin walk on the Moon.

1970

April
Apollo 13 narrowly escapes disaster.

1959

Project Mercury test launches begin.

1961

April 12 Cosmonaut Yuri Gagarin orbits Earth.

May 5 Alan Shepard becomes the first American in space.

May 25 President Kennedy announces the United States' goal to land on the Moon by the end of the 1960s.

1966

Project Gemini astronauts perfect docking and spacewalking.

1967

January 2 A launchpad fire claims the lives of three astronauts.

April 23 *Soyuz 1* crashes, killing all crew members.

Unmanned test launches of *Apollo* spacecraft are performed.

1971–1972

Four Apollo missions (14, 15, 16, 17) study lunar geology.

1973–1974

Skylab hosts manned scientific missions.

1975

July
The Apollo-Soyuz Test Project brings the U.S. and Soviet space programs together for the first time.

LIVING HISTORY

Primary sources provide firsthand evidence about a topic. Witnesses to a historical event create primary sources. They include autobiographies, newspaper reports of the time, oral histories, photographs, and memoirs. A secondary source analyzes primary sources, and is one step or more removed from the event. Secondary sources include textbooks, encyclopedias, and commentaries.

The *Apollo-Soyuz* Docking The docking of U.S. and Soviet spacecraft marked the end of the space race. Watch a video of the docking by visiting *www.nasa.gov/topics/history/features/astp_35 .html*

The First Space Walk Alexei Leonov made history when he became the first man to complete a space walk. Watch a video of the space walk by visiting *http://spaceflight.nasa.gov/history/shuttle-mir /multimedia/video/v-007.mpg*

***Friendship 7* Liftoff** John Glenn became a national hero when he orbited Earth. Watch CBS's coverage of the event by visiting *www.cbsnews.com/video/watch/?id=3311711n*

The Moon Landing The 1969 Moon landing is one of the most important events of the space race. Watch video footage of the *Apollo 11* launch and the Moon landing by visiting *www.youtube .com/watch?v=oDtWnCSsBSQ&feature=related*

The Science Advisory Committee Report on the Nuclear Age This 1957 report on national defense frightened the nation by declaring that the Soviet Union could attack with nuclear weapons at any time. Read the entire report by visiting *www.gwu.edu/~nsarchiv /NSAEBB/NSAEBB139/nitze02.pdf*

RESOURCES

Books

Chaikin, Andrew. *Mission Control, This Is Apollo: The Story of the First Voyages to the Moon.* New York: Viking Juvenile, 2009.

Dyer, Alan. *Mission to the Moon.* New York: Simon & Schuster Children's Publishing, 2009.

Stott, Carole. *Space Exploration.* New York: DK Children, 2004.

Thimmesh, Catherine. *Team Moon: How 400,000 People Landed* Apollo 11 *on the Moon.* Boston: Houghton Mifflin Books for Children, 2006.

Watkins, Billy, and Fred Haise. *Apollo Moon Missions: The Unsung Heroes.* Lincoln, NE: Bison Books, 2007.

Web Sites

History.com—The Space Race

www.history.com/topics/space-race

Watch videos and read articles about the space race.

NASA

www.nasa.gov

Visit the official NASA Web site to learn more about what the U.S. space program is working on today.

Smithsonian National Air and Space Museum

www.nasm.si.edu/

The National Air and Space Museum features a wide variety of exhibits dealing with the history of space exploration.

Visit this Scholastic Web site for more information on the space race: www.factsfornow.scholastic.com

GLOSSARY

air lock (AIR LAHK) a device that keeps air pressure from changing inside of a spacecraft

altitude (AL-ti-tood) the height of something above the ground or above sea level

communism (KAHM-yuh-niz-uhm) a way of organizing the economy of a country so that all the land, property, businesses, and resources belong to the government or community, and the profits are shared by all

docking (DAHK-ing) the connection of two spacecraft

fuel cells (FYOO-uhl SELZ) devices that create energy by changing hydrogen and oxygen into water

lunar (LOO-nur) having to do with the Moon

Mach (MAHK) a unit for measuring speed, often used for aircraft

navigation (nav-i-GAY-shuhn) finding where you are and where you need to go when you travel in a ship, an aircraft, or other vehicle

orbit (OR-bit) the curved path followed by a moon, planet, or satellite as it circles another planet or the Sun

propaganda (prah-puh-GAN-duh) information that is spread to influence the way people think, to gain supporters, or to damage an opposing group

rendezvous (RAHN-day-voo) appointment to meet at a certain time or place

rockets (RAH-kits) tube-shaped vehicles, propelled by very powerful engines, that are designed for traveling through space or carrying missiles

supersonic (soo-pur-SAH-nik) at or having to do with a speed faster than that of sound

INDEX

Page numbers in *italics* indicate illustrations.

ABOUT THE AUTHOR

Peter Benoit is a graduate of Skidmore College in Saratoga Springs, New York. His degree is in mathematics. He has been a tutor and educator for many years. Peter has written more than two dozen books for Children's Press. He has written about ecosystems, disasters, and Native Americans, among other topics. He is also the author of more than 2,000 poems.